C000078464

COLOGNE
RESTAURANT GUIDE

RESTAURANTS, BARS AND CAFES
Your Guide to Authentic Regional Eats

GUIDE BOOK FOR TOURIST

COLOGNE RESTAURANT GUIDE 2022
Best Rated Restaurants in Cologne, Germany

© Richard H. Villeneuve
© E.G.P. Editorial

Printed in USA.

ISBN-13: 9798500422064

COLOGNE RESTAURANT GUIDE

The Most Recommended Restaurants in Cologne

This directory is dedicated to the Business Owners and Managers who provide the experience that the locals and tourists enjoy. Thanks you very much for all that you do and thank for being the "People Choice".

Thanks to everyone that posts their reviews online and the amazing reviews sites that make our life easier.

The places listed in this book are the most positively reviewed and recommended by locals and travelers from around the world.

Thank you for your time and enjoy the directory that is designed with locals and tourist in mind!

TOP 500
RESTAURANTS
Ranked from #1 to #500

#1
Lommerzheim
Cuisines: Dive Bar, Gastropub
Average price: Modest
Area: Deutz
Address: Siegesstr. 18
50679 Cologne Germany
Phone: 0221 814392

#2
Toscanini
Cuisines: Italian, Pizza
Average price: Modest
Area: Severinsviertel
Address: Jakobstr. 22
50678 Cologne Germany
Phone: 0221 3109990

#3
Kaizen
Cuisines: Japanese
Average price: Expensive
Area: Rathenauviertel
Address: Lindenstr. 67
50674 Cologne Germany
Phone: 0221 16915037

#4
Villa Mathilde
Cuisines: Cafe
Average price: Modest
Area: Deutz
Address: Mathildenstr. 27
50679 Cologne Germany
Phone: 0221 99449496

#5
Bei Oma Kleinmann
Cuisines: Gastropub, German
Average price: Modest
Area: Rathenauviertel
Address: Zülpicher Str. 9
50674 Cologne Germany
Phone: 0221 232346

#6
Maison Blue
Cuisines: French, Wine Bar
Average price: Expensive
Area: Severinsviertel
Address: Im Ferkulum 18-22
50678 Cologne Germany
Phone: 0221 9328996

#7
La Société
Cuisines: French
Average price: Exclusive
Area: Rathenauviertel
Address: Kyffhäuserstr. 53
50674 Cologne Germany
Phone: 0221 232464

#8
Cafe Wohnraum
Cuisines: Cafe
Average price: Modest
Area: Nippes
Address: Neusser Str. 314
50733 Cologne Germany
Phone: 0176 39512505

#9
Bulgogi-Haus
Cuisines: Korean
Average price: Modest
Area: Weidenpesch
Address: Neusser Str. 654
50737 Cologne Germany
Phone: 0221 2788896

#10
Haus Scholzen
Cuisines: German
Average price: Expensive
Area: Ehrenfeld
Address: Venloer Str. 236
50823 Cologne Germany
Phone: 0221 515919

#11
Pizzeria Il Futuro
Cuisines: Pizza, Italian
Average price: Modest
Area: Kalk
Address: Johann-Mayer-Str. 1
51105 Cologne Germany
Phone: 0221 8708473

#12
Heimisch
Cuisines: Cafe
Average price: Inexpensive
Area: Deutz
Address: Deutzer Freiheit 72
50679 Cologne Germany
Phone: 0221 16838563

#13
Restaurant Meson El Cordobes
Cuisines: Spanish, German
Average price: Modest
Area: Belgisches Viertel
Address: Gladbacher Str. 11
50672 Cologne Germany
Phone: 0221 515506

#14
Beirut
Cuisines: Lebanese
Average price: Modest
Area: Martinsviertel
Address: Buttermarkt 3
50667 Cologne Germany
Phone: 0221 2581539

#15
Cafe Wahlen
Cuisines: German, Cafe
Average price: Modest
Area: Mauritiusviertel
Address: Hohenstaufenring 64
50674 Cologne Germany
Phone: 0221 231625

#16
Freddy Schilling
Cuisines: Burgers, Food Stand
Average price: Modest
Area: Rathenauviertel
Address: Kyffhäuserstr. 34
50674 Cologne Germany
Phone: 0221 16955515

#17
Jan's Restaurant in der Remise
Cuisines: French
Average price: Expensive
Area: Müngersdorf
Address: Wendelinstr. 48
50933 Cologne Germany
Phone: 0221 5103999

#18
Freddy Schilling
Cuisines: Burgers
Average price: Modest
Area: Eigelstein
Address: Eigelstein 147
50668 Cologne Germany
Phone: 0221 16894447

#19
Habibi
Cuisines: Middle Eastern, Arabian
Average price: Inexpensive
Area: Rathenauviertel
Address: Zülpicher Str. 28
50674 Cologne Germany
Phone: 0221 2717141

#20
Shaka Zulu
Cuisines: African, Cocktail Bar
Average price: Modest
Area: Belgisches Viertel
Address: Limburger Str. 29
50672 Cologne Germany
Phone: 0221 16862814

#21
Restaurant Brücken
Cuisines: German
Average price: Modest
Area: Kunibertsviertel
Address: Johannisstr. 79
50668 Cologne Germany
Phone: 0221 37994830

#22
Non La
Cuisines: Vietnamese
Average price: Modest
Area: Belgisches Viertel
Address: Aachener Str. 31
50674 Cologne Germany
Phone: 0221 2572298

#23
Hommage
Cuisines: Cafe, Creperies, Coffee & Tea
Average price: Inexpensive
Area: Gereonsviertel
Address: Friesenstr. 75
50670 Cologne Germany
Phone: 0178 1022416

#24
Zum Köbes
Cuisines: Dive Bar, Rhinelandian
Average price: Modest
Area: Kunibertsviertel
Address: Clever Str. 2
50668 Cologne Germany
Phone: 0221 80064548

#25
Engelbät
Cuisines: Bar, Creperies,
Breakfast & Brunch
Average price: Modest
Area: Kwatier Latäng
Address: Engelbertstr. 7
50674 Cologne Germany
Phone: 0221 246914

#26
Pasta Bar
Cuisines: Italian
Average price: Modest
Area: Pantaleonsviertel
Address: Salierring 46
50677 Cologne Germany
Phone: 0221 9386311

#27
La Barra
Cuisines: Bar, Tapas Bar
Average price: Modest
Area: Mauritiusviertel
Address: Barbarossaplatz 8
50674 Cologne Germany
Phone: 0221 4232203

#28
Haus Schwan
Cuisines: German
Average price: Modest
Area: Lindenthal
Address: Dürener Str. 235
50931 Cologne Germany
Phone: 0221 403368

#29
Miss Päpki
Cuisines: Cafe
Average price: Modest
Area: Belgisches Viertel
Address: Brüsseler Platz 18
50674 Cologne Germany
Phone: 0221 16834971

#30
Tom Yam Gung
Cuisines: Thai
Average price: Inexpensive
Area: Rathenauviertel
Address: Kyffhäuserstr. 52
50674 Cologne Germany
Phone: 0221 27225939

#31
Khun Mae
Cuisines: Thai, Food Stand
Average price: Inexpensive
Area: Rathenauviertel
Address: Kyffhäuserstr. 38
50674 Cologne Germany
Phone: 0221 39757759

#33
Daikan
Cuisines: Ramen, Tapas Bar
Average price: Expensive
Area: Belgisches Viertel
Address: Maastrichter Str. 9
50672 Cologne Germany
Phone: 0221 30135906

#32
Puszta Hütte
Cuisines: Hungarian, German
Average price: Inexpensive
Area: Cäcilienviertel
Address: Fleischmengergasse 57
50676 Cologne Germany
Phone: 0221 239471

#34
**El Inca Restaurante
Latino Americano**
Cuisines: Latin American
Average price: Modest
Area: Rathenauviertel
Address: Görresstr. 2
50674 Cologne Germany
Phone: 0221 245503

#35
Noa
Cuisines: Cafe, International
Average price: Modest
Area: Belgisches Viertel
Address: Maastrichter Str. 3
50672 Cologne Germany
Phone: 0221 16811101

#36
Mercato Deluxe
Cuisines: Italian
Average price: Expensive
Area: Eigelstein
Address: Bremer Str. 5
50670 Cologne Germany
Phone: 0221 1399474

#37
Brauerei zur Malzmühle
Cuisines: Brewery, German
Average price: Modest
Area: Georgsviertel
Address: Heumarkt 6
50667 Cologne Germany
Phone: 0221 92160613

#38
Lu Vietnamese Cuisine
Cuisines: Vietnamese
Average price: Modest
Area: Kwatier Latäng
Address: Hohenstaufenring 21
50674 Cologne Germany
Phone: 0221 54813457

#39
Namdaemun
Cuisines: Korean
Average price: Modest
Area: Südstadt
Address: Bonner Str. 75
50677 Cologne Germany
Phone: 0221 99200051

#40
Gasthaus Brungs
Cuisines: Beer Garden, German
Average price: Expensive
Area: Martinsviertel
Address: Marsplatz 3-5
50667 Cologne Germany
Phone: 0221 2581666

#41
Signor Verde
Cuisines: Vegan, Cafe
Average price: Modest
Area: Rathenauviertel
Address: Otto-Fischer-Str. 1
50674 Cologne Germany
Phone: 0163 8436654

#42
Cu'd'oro
Cuisines: Cafe, Breakfast & Brunch
Average price: Inexpensive
Area: Agnesviertel
Address: Krefelder Str. 7
50670 Cologne Germany
Phone: 0221 58475665

#43
Der Goldfisch
Cuisines: Greek
Average price: Modest
Area: Ehrenfeld
Address: Subbelrather Str. 221
50823 Cologne Germany
Phone: 0221 16997854

#44
Trash-Chic
Cuisines: Dive Bar, Vegetarian
Average price: Inexpensive
Area: Kalk
Address: Wiersbergstr. 31
51103 Cologne Germany
Phone: 0221 82822968

#45
Speisekammer
Cuisines: Cafe, International
Average price: Modest
Area: Südstadt
Address: Alteburger Str. 18
50678 Cologne Germany
Phone: 0221 16857386

#46
Gado Gado
Cuisines: International, Indonesian
Average price: Modest
Area: Belgisches Viertel
Address: Gladbacher Str. 31
50672 Cologne Germany
Phone: 0221 94654101

#47
Ginger Restaurant
Cuisines: Chinese
Average price: Modest
Area: Gereonsviertel
Address: Steinfelder Gasse 1
50670 Cologne Germany
Phone: 0221 16924913

#48
Meister Gerhard
Cuisines: Tapas Bar
Average price: Modest
Area: Rathenauviertel
Address: Rathenauplatz 8
50674 Cologne Germany
Phone: 0221 39757650

#49
Herings im Martinswinkel
Cuisines: Seafood, German
Average price: Modest
Area: Martinsviertel
Address: Fischmarkt 9
50667 Cologne Germany
Phone: 0221 2575751

#50
Gaststätte Max Stark
Cuisines: German
Average price: Modest
Area: Kunibertsviertel
Address: Unter Kahlenhausen 47
50668 Cologne Germany
Phone: 0221 2005633

#51
Braustelle
Cuisines: Brewery, Gastropub
Average price: Modest
Area: Ehrenfeld
Address: Christianstr. 2
50825 Cologne Germany
Phone: 0221 2856932

#52
Sorgenfrei Wein und Speisen
Cuisines: Wine Bar, International
Average price: Expensive
Area: Belgisches Viertel
Address: Antwerpener Str. 15
50672 Cologne Germany
Phone: 0221 3557327

#53
Meat.ing
Cuisines: Korean
Average price: Expensive
Area: Georgsviertel
Address: Hohe Pforte 9-11
50676 Cologne Germany
Phone: 0221 99556860

#54
Fellini
Cuisines: Italian
Average price: Expensive
Area: Sülz
Address: Zülpicher Str. 327
50937 Cologne Germany
Phone: 0221 441900

#55
Reissdorf em Keuchhof
Cuisines: Rhinelandian, Beer Garden
Average price: Modest
Area: Lövenich
Address: Braugasse 12 - 14
50859 Cologne Germany
Phone: 02234 47202

#56
Le PomPom
Cuisines: Cafe, Cupcakes
Average price: Modest
Area: Belgisches Viertel
Address: Lindenstr. 38
50674 Cologne Germany
Phone: 0221 96308166

#57
Momotaro
Cuisines: Japanese, Sushi Bar
Average price: Expensive
Area: Apostelnviertel
Address: Benesisstr. 56
50672 Cologne Germany
Phone: 0221 2571432

#58
Die Rösterei
Cuisines: Cafe, Coffee Roasteries
Average price: Modest
Area: Belgisches Viertel
Address: Aachener Str. 22
50674 Cologne Germany
Phone: 0221 5894179

#59
Karl Hermann's
Cuisines: Burgers, Bar
Average price: Modest
Area: Ehrenfeld
Address: Venloer Str. 538
50825 Cologne Germany
Phone: 0221 59557960

#60
Pizza per Tutti
Cuisines: Italian, Pizza
Average price: Inexpensive
Area: Sülz
Address: Zülpicher Str. 231
50937 Cologne Germany
Phone: 0221 419595

#61
Mangal
Cuisines: Turkish
Average price: Modest
Area: Eigelstein
Address: Weidengasse 58 - 62
50668 Cologne Germany
Phone: 0221 29883420

#62
Pizzeria Caminetto
Cuisines: Pizza, Italian
Average price: Inexpensive
Area: Volksgartenviertel
Address: Eifelstr. 37
50677 Cologne Germany
Phone: 0221 3104664

#63
Rheinau
Cuisines: Bar, German
Average price: Modest
Area: Severinsviertel
Address: Im Siontal 2
50678 Cologne Germany
Phone: 0221 99701230

#64
Peters Brauhaus
Cuisines: German, Gastropub
Average price: Modest
Area: Martinsviertel
Address: Mühlengasse 1
50667 Cologne Germany
Phone: 0221 2573950

#65
Früh am Dom
Cuisines: Beer Garden, German, Brewery
Average price: Modest
Area: Martinsviertel
Address: Am Hof 12-18
50667 Cologne Germany
Phone: 0221 2613215

#66
Los Navarros
Cuisines: Cafe, Bistro, Spanish
Average price: Modest
Area: Südstadt
Address: Merowingerstr. 43
50677 Cologne Germany
Phone: 0172 7457106

#67
Shibuya Sushi
Cuisines: Sushi Bar,
Japanese, Lounges
Average price: Modest
Area: Nippes
Address: Neusser Str. 332
50733 Cologne Germany
Phone: 0221 30145045

#68
WeinAmRhein
Cuisines: European, Wine Bar
Average price: Expensive
Area: Kunibertsviertel
Address: Johannisstr. 64
50668 Cologne Germany
Phone: 0221 91248885

#69
Olympia Grill
Cuisines: Greek
Average price: Inexpensive
Area: Mauenheim
Address: Friedrich-Karl-Str. 30
50739 Cologne Germany
Phone: 0221 7407447

#70
Brauhaus Pütz
Cuisines: Gastropub
Average price: Modest
Area: Belgisches Viertel
Address: Engelbertstr. 67
50674 Cologne Germany
Phone: 0221 211166

#71
Weinhaus Vogel
Cuisines: German
Average price: Inexpensive
Area: Eigelstein
Address: Eigelstein 74
50668 Cologne Germany
Phone: 0221 1399134

#72
Black Karate
Cuisines: Japanese,
Chinese, Sushi Bar
Average price: Modest
Area: Gereonsviertel
Address: Friesenwall 116
50672 Cologne Germany
Phone: 0221 28068790

#73
Cafe Fridolin
Cuisines: Cafe
Average price: Inexpensive
Area: Ehrenfeld
Address: Venloer Str. 425
50825 Cologne Germany
Phone: 01575 9045819

#74
La Tasca
Cuisines: Portuguese
Average price: Modest
Area: Weiden
Address: Aachener Str. 1130
50858 Cologne Germany
Phone: 02234 9495888

#75
Zen
Cuisines: Japanese, Sushi Bar
Average price: Expensive
Area: Lindenthal
Address: Bachemer Str. 236
50935 Cologne Germany
Phone: 0221 28285755

#76
Restaurant Kilim
Cuisines: Turkish
Average price: Modest
Area: Mülheim
Address: Keupstr. 69
51063 Cologne Germany
Phone: 0221 616597

#77
Lo Sfizio
Cuisines: Italian, Specialty Food
Average price: Modest
Area: Agnesviertel
Address: Hansaring 149
50670 Cologne Germany
Phone: 0221 16890449

#78
Schwimmbad Rhein-Sommergarten
Cuisines: Beer Garden
Average price: Inexpensive
Area: Riehl
Address: An der Schanz 2 a
50735 Cologne Germany
Phone: 0221 7602843

#79
Dreiundsiebziger
Cuisines: Mediterranean, International
Average price: Modest
Area: Belgisches Viertel
Address: Limburger Str. 19
50672 Cologne Germany
Phone: 0221 16832420

#80
Gogi Matcha
Cuisines: Korean
Average price: Modest
Area: Kunibertsviertel
Address: Johannisstr. 47
50668 Cologne Germany
Phone: 0221 72024255

#81
Vielfalt Tapas
Cuisines: Cafe, Wine Bar, Tapas Bar
Average price: Modest
Area: Neuehrenfeld
Address: Lenauplatz 9
50825 Cologne Germany
Phone: 0221 3552250

#82
Mandalay
Cuisines: Burmese
Average price: Modest
Area: Belgisches Viertel
Address: Brüsseler Str. 53
50674 Cologne Germany
Phone: 0221 5101296

#83
Gilden im Zims
Cuisines: Brewery, German
Average price: Modest
Area: Martinsviertel
Address: Heumarkt 77
50667 Cologne Germany
Phone: 0221 16866110

#84
Le Moissonnier
Cuisines: French, Wine Bar
Average price: Exclusive
Area: Agnesviertel
Address: Krefelder Str. 25
50670 Cologne Germany
Phone: 0221 729479

#85
La Casona
Cuisines: Steakhouse
Average price: Modest
Area: Agnesviertel
Address: Riehler Str. 105
50668 Cologne Germany
Phone: 0221 70211008

#86
Beef Brothers
Cuisines: Burgers, Food Stand
Average price: Modest
Area: Belgisches Viertel
Address: Aachener Str. 12
50674 Cologne Germany
Phone: 0221 29834736

#87
Chang Thai
Cuisines: Thai, Fast Food
Average price: Inexpensive
Area: Sülz
Address: Berrenrather Str. 220
50939 Cologne Germany
Phone: 0221 29966093

#88
O sole mio
Cuisines: Pizza, Italian
Average price: Inexpensive
Area: Eigelstein
Address: Eintrachtstr. 6
50668 Cologne Germany
Phone: 0221 1300307

#89
Servus Colonia Alpina
Cuisines: Bavarian
Average price: Modest
Area: Martinsviertel
Address: Steinweg 12 - 14
50667 Cologne Germany
Phone: 0221 29219250

#90
Bande à Part
Cuisines: Creperies
Average price: Modest
Area: Severinsviertel
Address: Silvanstr. 1
50678 Cologne Germany
Phone: 0221 33879595

#91
Tapeo Picus
Cuisines: Tapas Bar, Cocktail Bar
Average price: Modest
Area: Lindenthal
Address: Classen-Kappelmann-Str. 25-27
50931 Cologne Germany
Phone: 0221 82082000

#92
Pane e Cioccolata
Cuisines: Italian
Average price: Modest
Area: Neuehrenfeld
Address: Jessestr. 2
50823 Cologne Germany
Phone: 0221 558996

#93
Grillstube Pizzeria
Cuisines: Food Stand, Pizza
Average price: Inexpensive
Area: Mülheim
Address: Alte Wipperfürther Str. 72
51065 Cologne Germany
Phone: 0221 695619

#94
Sushi-Haus
Cuisines: Sushi Bar
Average price: Modest
Area: Deutz
Address: Von-Sandt-Platz 12
50679 Cologne Germany
Phone: 0221 88754515

#95
Meer sehen
Cuisines: Pubs, International
Average price: Modest
Area: Ehrenfeld
Address: Philippstr. 1
50823 Cologne Germany
Phone: 0221 9923149

#96
Bay Area Burrito Company
Cuisines: Mexican, Tex-Mex, Vegetarian
Average price: Modest
Area: Apostelnviertel
Address: Friesenwall 16
50672 Cologne Germany
Phone: 0221 16823024

#97
Thiebolds Eck
Cuisines: Pubs, German
Average price: Inexpensive
Area: Cäcilienviertel
Address: Lungengasse 31
50676 Cologne Germany
Phone: 0221 214434

#98
Belgischer Hof
Cuisines: Brasseries, French, Belgian
Average price: Modest
Area: Belgisches Viertel
Address: Brüsseler Str. 54
50674 Cologne Germany
Phone: 0221 54817017

#99
Café Elefant
Cuisines: Cafe
Average price: Modest
Area: Agnesviertel
Address: Weißenburgstr. 50
50670 Cologne Germany
Phone: 0221 734520

#100
Chinarestaurant Lei Lei
Cuisines: Chinese
Average price: Modest
Area: Gereonsviertel
Address: Hansaring 22
50670 Cologne Germany
Phone: 0221 131772

#101
Palanta
Cuisines: International
Average price: Modest
Area: Sülz
Address: Sülzburgstr. 193
50937 Cologne Germany
Phone: 0221 29784711

#102
Dank Augusta
Cuisines: Cafe
Average price: Modest
Area: Riehl
Address: Am Botanischen Garten 1a
50735 Cologne Germany
Phone: 0221 2848488

#103
Zeit Für Brot
Cuisines: Bakery, Cafe
Average price: Inexpensive
Area: Ehrenfeld
Address: Venloer Str. 202
50823 Cologne Germany
Phone: 0221 17074800

#104
Grand The Sushi Circle
Cuisines: Sushi Bar, Japanese
Average price: Modest
Area: Belgisches Viertel
Address: Lütticher Str. 7
50674 Cologne Germany
Phone: 0221 27249328

#105
Haptilu
Cuisines: Bistro, Breakfast & Brunch, Cafe
Average price: Modest
Area: Severinsviertel
Address: Kartäuserhof 2   ·
50678 Cologne Germany
Phone: 0221 9983486

#106
Hase Restaurant
Cuisines: French, Mediterranean, Italian
Average price: Expensive
Area: Gereonsviertel
Address: St.-Apern-Str. 17
50667 Cologne Germany
Phone: 0221 254375

#107
Dostoevsky
Cuisines: Russian, Bar, Cafe
Average price: Modest
Area: Rathenauviertel
Address: Barbarossaplatz 3-5
50674 Cologne Germany
Phone: 0221 93118420

#108
Spencer & Hill
Cuisines: Italian
Average price: Modest
Area: Apostelnviertel
Address: Hohenzollernring 16 - 18
50672 Cologne Germany
Phone: 0221 280646362

#109
Thai Food
Cuisines: Thai
Average price: Inexpensive
Area: Belgisches Viertel
Address: Hohenzollernring 27
50672 Cologne Germany
Phone: 0221 27799579

#110
Marcellino
Cuisines: Italian
Average price: Expensive
Area: Agnesviertel
Address: Krefelder Str. 39
50670 Cologne Germany
Phone: 0221 99878320

#111
Keimaks
Cuisines: Bar, Bistro
Average price: Modest
Area: Südstadt
Address: Kurfürstenstr. 27
50678 Cologne Germany
Phone: 0221 312670

#112
Da Enzo
Cuisines: Italian
Average price: Modest
Area: Mülheim
Address: Regentenstr. 9
51063 Cologne Germany
Phone: 0221 623478

#113
Sweet Sushi
Cuisines: Japanese, Sushi Bar
Average price: Modest
Area: Neumarkt Viertel
Address: Auf dem Berlich 11
50667 Cologne Germany
Phone: 0221 29026985

#114
Café Sehnsucht
Cuisines: Cafe, European
Average price: Modest
Area: Ehrenfeld
Address: Körnerstr. 67
50823 Cologne Germany
Phone: 0221 528347

#115
Grilletta Salamis
Cuisines: Greek
Average price: Modest
Area: Sülz
Address: Blankenheimer Str. 2
50937 Cologne Germany
Phone: 0221 4759955

#116
Mangia e vai
Cuisines: Pizza
Average price: Modest
Area: Belgisches Viertel
Address: Roonstr. 88
50674 Cologne Germany
Phone: 0221 494949

#117
Lakshmi
Cuisines: Indian
Average price: Inexpensive
Area: Cäcilienviertel
Address: Thieboldsgasse 101-103
50676 Cologne Germany
Phone: 0221 3500802

#118
epicerie boucherie
Cuisines: Specialty Food, French
Average price: Modest
Area: Südstadt
Address: Elsaßstr. 3
50677 Cologne Germany
Phone: 0221 31081999

#119
Odonien
Cuisines: Music Venues, Beer Garden
Average price: Modest
Area: Neuehrenfeld
Address: Hornstr. 85
50823 Cologne Germany
Phone: 0221 9727009

#120
A Caravela
Cuisines: Portuguese, Seafood
Average price: Modest
Area: Mauritiusviertel
Address: Weyerstr. 61
50676 Cologne Germany
Phone: 0221 245483

#121
Brehmer's Conditorei
Cuisines: Patisserie/Cake Shop, Cafe,
Breakfast & Brunch
Average price: Inexpensive
Area: Merheim
Address: Olpener Str. 417
51109 Cologne Germany
Phone: 0221 896131

#122
Rich 'n Greens
Cuisines: Mexican
Average price: Inexpensive
Area: Neumarkt Viertel
Address: Auf dem Berlich 9
50667 Cologne Germany
Phone: 0221 84639530

#123
Petit Noir
Cuisines: Cafe, Coffee & Tea
Average price: Inexpensive
Area: Sülz
Address: Weyertal 42
50937 Cologne Germany
Phone: 0221 2825737

#124
Hahnheiser
Cuisines: German
Average price: Modest
Area: Nippes
Address: Yorckstr. 32
50733 Cologne Germany
Phone: 0221 7601898

#125
Taverne Alekos
Cuisines: Greek
Average price: Modest
Area: Ehrenfeld
Address: Venloer Str. 275
50823 Cologne Germany
Phone: 0221 516640

#126
Salute
Cuisines: Pizza
Average price: Modest
Area: Lindenthal
Address: Lindenthalgürtel 54
50935 Cologne Germany
Phone: 0221 4069099

#127
Sonnim
Cuisines: Korean
Average price: Modest
Area: Kwatier Latäng
Address: Hohenstaufenring 14
50674 Cologne Germany
Phone: 0221 16873320

#128
Fromanda
Cuisines: Chinese
Average price: Modest
Area: Nippes
Address: Florastr. 174
50733 Cologne Germany
Phone: 0221 99719762

#129
Ni Hao China Imbiss Take-Away
Cuisines: Chinese
Average price: Inexpensive
Area: Belgisches Viertel
Address: Brüsseler Str. 44
50674 Cologne Germany
Phone: 0221 251815

#130
Stern am Rathaus
Cuisines: Cafe
Average price: Modest
Area: Martinsviertel
Address: Bürgerstr. 6
50667 Cologne Germany
Phone: 0221 22251750

#131
The Bistro
Cuisines: Bistro
Average price: Modest
Area: Kunibertsviertel
Address: Dagobertstr. 23
50668 Cologne Germany
Phone: 0221 846330

#132
Krua Thai
Cuisines: Thai
Average price: Inexpensive
Area: Belgisches Viertel
Address: Brüsseler Str. 40 - 42
50674 Cologne Germany
Phone: 0221 2774636

#133
Com Pho
Cuisines: Vietnamese
Average price: Inexpensive
Area: Rathenauviertel
Address: Zülpicher Str. 58 D
50674 Cologne Germany
Phone: 0221 29780485

#134
Celentano
Cuisines: Italian
Average price: Modest
Area: Agnesviertel
Address: Maybachstr. 148
50670 Cologne Germany
Phone: 0221 7393004

#135
La Teca
Cuisines: Italian
Average price: Expensive
Area: Volksgartenviertel
Address: Eifelplatz 2
50677 Cologne Germany
Phone: 0221 313485

#136
Osman Bey
Cuisines: Turkish, Kebab
Average price: Inexpensive
Area: Severinsviertel
Address: Chlodwigplatz 16
50678 Cologne Germany
Phone: 0221 60607885

#137
Bagatelle
Cuisines: French
Average price: Modest
Area: Südstadt
Address: Teutoburger Str. 17
50678 Cologne Germany
Phone: 0160 99445267

#138
Lai de Hao
Cuisines: Chinese
Average price: Modest
Area: Pantaleonsviertel
Address: Salierring 38
50677 Cologne Germany
Phone: 0221 2053336

#139
Taco Loco Restaurant
Cuisines: American, Mexican, Cocktail Bar
Average price: Modest
Area: Müngersdorf
Address: Aachenerstr. 702
50933 Cologne Germany
Phone: 0221 2714411

#140
Mirai Sushi
Cuisines: Sushi Bar, Japanese, Vietnamese
Average price: Modest
Area: Mauritiusviertel
Address: Hahnenstr. 25
50676 Cologne Germany
Phone: 0221 16844084

#141
Cafecafe
Cuisines: Breakfast & Brunch, Cafe
Average price: Modest
Area: Belgisches Viertel
Address: Aachener Str. 45
50674 Cologne Germany
Phone: 0221 2706639

#142
Limani
Cuisines: Mediterranean, Greek
Average price: Modest
Area: Südstadt
Address: Agrippinawerft 6
50678 Cologne Germany
Phone: 0221 7190590

#143
Vasco da Gama
Cuisines: Portuguese
Average price: Modest
Area: Neuehrenfeld
Address: Liebigstr. 120
50823 Cologne Germany
Phone: 0221 3566566

#144
Capricorn i Aries
Cuisines: French
Average price: Expensive
Area: Südstadt
Address: Alteburger Str. 31
50678 Cologne Germany
Phone: 0221 3975710

#145
Em Dörp
Cuisines: German
Average price: Modest
Area: Müngersdorf
Address: Vitalisstr. 389-391
50933 Cologne Germany
Phone: 0221 17076589

#146
Restaurant Amabile
Cuisines: French
Average price: Expensive
Area: Rathenauviertel
Address: Görresstr. 2
50674 Cologne Germany
Phone: 0221 219101

#147
Hoai Viet
Cuisines: Vietnamese, Thai
Average price: Inexpensive
Area: Eigelstein
Address: Weidengasse 68
50668 Cologne Germany
Phone: 0221 1393093

#148
La Gustosa
Cuisines: Italian
Average price: Modest
Area: Agnesviertel
Address: Sudermanplatz 6
50670 Cologne Germany
Phone: 0221 37998577

#149
Sankt Petersburg
Cuisines: Russian, Cafe,
Patisserie/Cake Shop
Average price: Modest
Area: Zollstock
Address: Höninger Weg 369
50969 Cologne Germany
Phone: 0221 75985705

#150
Iltis-Grill
Cuisines: German, Greek
Average price: Inexpensive
Area: Neuehrenfeld
Address: Iltisstr. 162
50825 Cologne Germany
Phone: 0221 5506377

#151
Antik Brauhaus
Cuisines: Dive Bar, Gastropub
Average price: Modest
Area: Deutz
Address: Deutzer Freiheit 85 - 87
50679 Cologne Germany
Phone: 0221 816947

#152
Vini Diretti
Cuisines: Italian
Average price: Modest
Area: Müngersdorf
Address: Wendelinstr. 61
50933 Cologne Germany
Phone: 0221 9473375

#153
Cyclo
Cuisines: Vietnamese
Average price: Modest
Area: Martinsviertel
Address: Martinstr. 6 - 8
50667 Cologne Germany
Phone: 0221 2712088

#154
Bei dr Tant
Cuisines: Gastropub
Average price: Modest
Area: Neumarkt Viertel
Address: Cäcilienstr. 28
50667 Cologne Germany
Phone: 0221 2577360

#155
Teabox
Cuisines: Sushi Bar, Japanese
Average price: Modest
Area: Kunibertsviertel
Address: Domstr. 93
50668 Cologne Germany
Phone: 01520 6131523

#156
Barrios
Cuisines: Mexican, Cocktail Bar
Average price: Modest
Area: Belgisches Viertel
Address: Hohenzollernring 21-23
50672 Cologne Germany
Phone: 0221 2572200

#157
Hellers Volksgarten
Cuisines: Beer Garden
Average price: Modest
Area: Volksgartenviertel
Address: Volksgartenstr. 27
50677 Cologne Germany
Phone: 0221 382626

#158
Klaaf
Cuisines: Bistro
Average price: Modest
Area: Eigelstein
Address: Eigelstein 124
50668 Cologne Germany
Phone: 0221 133385

#159
Café Vreiheit
Cuisines: Cafe, European
Average price: Modest
Area: Mülheim
Address: Wallstr. 91
51063 Cologne Germany
Phone: 0221 9917793

#160
Höninger
Cuisines: Dive Bar, German
Average price: Modest
Area: Zollstock
Address: Herthastr. 68
50969 Cologne Germany
Phone: 0221 3685422

#161
Meti Thai
Cuisines: Thai, Cocktail Bar
Average price: Modest
Area: Brück
Address: Brücker Mauspfad 592
51109 Cologne Germany
Phone: 0221 89060555

#162
Zur alten Zollgrenze
Cuisines: German
Average price: Modest
Area: Weidenpesch
Address: Neusser Str. 549
50737 Cologne Germany
Phone: 0221 748343

#163
Brasserie Fou
Cuisines: French, Asian Fusion,
Breakfast & Brunch
Average price: Expensive
Area: Kunibertsviertel
Address: Johannisstr. 76 - 80
50668 Cologne Germany
Phone: 0221 942220

#164
Alcazar
Cuisines: Dive Bar, International
Average price: Modest
Area: Belgisches Viertel
Address: Bismarckstr. 39 A
50672 Cologne Germany
Phone: 0221 515733

#165
Brauhaus Ohne Namen
Cuisines: Gastropub
Average price: Modest
Area: Deutz
Address: Mathildenstr. 42
50679 Cologne Germany
Phone: 0221 812680

#166
Zhing-Sam
Cuisines: Vietnamese, Thai
Average price: Modest
Area: Südstadt
Address: Sachsenring 3
50677 Cologne Germany
Phone: 0221 8014008

#167
Fink
Cuisines: European
Average price: Modest
Area: Nippes
Address: Siebachstr. 50
50733 Cologne Germany
Phone: 0221 78949989

#168
Casa Di Biase
Cuisines: Italian, Mediterranean
Average price: Expensive
Area: Volksgartenviertel
Address: Eifelplatz 4
50677 Cologne Germany
Phone: 0221 322433

#169
Casa di Modica
Cuisines: Italian
Average price: Expensive
Area: Apostelnviertel
Address: Friesenwall 104
50672 Cologne Germany
Phone: 0221 27799656

#170
Kamasutra
Cuisines: Indian
Average price: Expensive
Area: Mauritiusviertel
Address: Weyerstr. 114
50676 Cologne Germany
Phone: 0221 34892828

#171
Cafe LizBÄT
Cuisines: Creperies, Cafe
Average price: Modest
Area: Ehrenfeld
Address: Geisselstr. 6
50823 Cologne Germany
Phone: 0221 5104566

#172
La Bodega
Cuisines: Spanish, Tapas Bar
Average price: Modest
Area: Gereonsviertel
Address: Friesenstr. 51
50670 Cologne Germany
Phone: 0221 2573610

#173
Bona'me
Cuisines: Turkish, Oriental
Average price: Modest
Area: Deutz
Address: Kennedyplatz 2
50679 Cologne Germany
Phone: 0221 94999252

#174
Bona'me
Cuisines: Turkish
Average price: Modest
Area: Rheinauhafen
Address: Anna-Schneider-Steig 22
50678 Cologne Germany
Phone: 0221 39760407

#175
Restaurant Selam
Cuisines: Ethiopian
Average price: Modest
Area: Ehrenfeld
Address: Ehrenfeldgürtel 91
50823 Cologne Germany
Phone: 0221 9520352

#176
Stüsser's
Cuisines: German, Dive Bar
Average price: Modest
Area: Agnesviertel
Address: Neusser Str. 47
50670 Cologne Germany
Phone: 0221 47446999

#177
Sushiou
Cuisines: Japanese, Sushi Bar
Average price: Modest
Area: Gereonsviertel
Address: Christophstr. 41
50670 Cologne Germany
Phone: 0221 12062310

#178
Trattoria Stella
Cuisines: Italian
Average price: Modest
Area: Junkersdorf
Address: Kirchweg 7
50858 Cologne Germany
Phone: 0221 4849531

#179
Restaurant Lüchbaum
Cuisines: Italian
Average price: Modest
Area: Rodenkirchen
Address: Hauptstr. 61
50996 Cologne Germany
Phone: 0221 3779133

#180
Odessa
Cuisines: Russian
Average price: Modest
Area: Severinsviertel
Address: Im Ferkulum 32
50678 Cologne Germany
Phone: 0176 24761442

#181
Tacolonia
Cuisines: Mexican, Bar
Average price: Modest
Area: Nippes
Address: Kempener Str. 56
50733 Cologne Germany
Phone: 0221 723981

#182
Serithai
Cuisines: Thai
Average price: Modest
Area: Mauritiusviertel
Address: Schaafenstr. 63
50676 Cologne Germany
Phone: 0221 231969

#183
Restaurant Glashaus
Cuisines: European, Breakfast & Brunch
Average price: Expensive
Area: Deutz
Address: Hyatt Regency Cologne
50679 Cologne Germany
Phone: 0221 82811773

#184
Tokyo Sushi
Cuisines: Japanese, Sushi Bar
Average price: Modest
Area: Kwatier Latäng
Address: Roonstr. 8
50674 Cologne Germany
Phone: 0221 246239

#185
art'otel cologne by park plaza
Cuisines: Hotels, Cafe
Average price: Modest
Area: Rheinauhafen
Address: Holzmarkt 4
50676 Cologne Germany
Phone: 0221 801030

#186
Zimmermann's Burger
Cuisines: Burgers
Average price: Modest
Area: Belgisches Viertel
Address: Venloer Str. 39
50672 Cologne Germany
Phone: 0221 46755525

#187
MeiWok V
Cuisines: Vegan, Asian Fusion
Average price: Modest
Area: Ehrenfeld
Address: Venloer Str. 384
50825 Cologne Germany
Phone: 0221 96269707

#188
Restaurant Bali
Cuisines: Indonesian
Average price: Modest
Area: Belgisches Viertel
Address: Brüsseler Platz 2
50672 Cologne Germany
Phone: 0221 522914

#189
FRÜH "Em Veedel"
Cuisines: German, Gastropub
Average price: Modest
Area: Severinsviertel
Address: Chlodwigplatz 28
50678 Cologne Germany
Phone: 0221 314470

#190
Madame Miammiam
Cuisines: Cafe, Patisserie/Cake Shop
Average price: Expensive
Area: Belgisches Viertel
Address: Antwerpener Str. 39
50672 Cologne Germany
Phone: 0221 94998519

#191
Burgerlich
Cuisines: Burgers
Average price: Modest
Area: Belgisches Viertel
Address: Hohenzollernring 25
50672 Cologne Germany
Phone: 0221 27099966

#192
Stanton
Cuisines: Cafe
Average price: Modest
Area: Martinsviertel
Address: Schildergasse 57
50667 Cologne Germany
Phone: 0221 2710710

#193
Frittenwerk
Cuisines: Fast Food
Average price: Inexpensive
Area: Apostelnviertel
Address: Ehrenstr. 94
50672 Cologne Germany
Phone: 0211 97174369

#194
Fischermanns'
Cuisines: International
Average price: Expensive
Area: Rathenauviertel
Address: Rathenauplatz 21
50674 Cologne Germany
Phone: 0221 8017790

#195
485grad
Cuisines: Pizza, Wine Bar
Average price: Modest
Area: Rathenauviertel
Address: Kyffhäuserstr. 44
50674 Cologne Germany
Phone: 0221 39753330

#196
El Chango
Cuisines: Argentine, Steakhouse
Average price: Expensive
Area: Martinsviertel
Address: Bolzengasse 9
50667 Cologne Germany
Phone: 0221 2581212

#197
Beijing
Cuisines: Chinese
Average price: Modest
Area: Lindenthal
Address: Lindenthalgürtel 62
50935 Cologne Germany
Phone: 0221 4061411

#198
Brauhaus Reissdorf
Cuisines: Gastropub, Rhinelandian, Bowling
Average price: Modest
Area: Cäcilienviertel
Address: Kleiner Griechenmarkt 40
50676 Cologne Germany
Phone: 0221 219254

#199
Murat
Cuisines: Kebab, Pizza
Average price: Inexpensive
Area: Ehrenfeld
Address: Venloer Str. 464
50825 Cologne Germany
Phone: 0221 5502703

#200
Sünner Keller
Cuisines: German, Brewery
Average price: Modest
Area: Kalk
Address: Kalker Hauptstr. 260 - 262
51103 Cologne Germany
Phone: 0221 98557400

#201
Limbourg
Cuisines: French, Mediterranean
Average price: Modest
Area: Belgisches Viertel
Address: Limburger Str. 35
50672 Cologne Germany
Phone: 0221 2508880

#202
Flüssiggold
Cuisines: Cafe, Breakfast & Brunch
Average price: Modest
Area: Mauritiusviertel
Address: Hohenstaufenring 58
50674 Cologne Germany
Phone: 0221 16875530

#203
Piccola Essen & Trinken
Cuisines: Italian
Average price: Modest
Area: Ehrenfeld
Address: Venloer Str. 410-412
50825 Cologne Germany
Phone: 0221 5402360

#204
Die Wohngemeinschaft
Cuisines: Bar, Cafe, Hostels
Average price: Modest
Area: Belgisches Viertel
Address: Richard-Wagner-Str. 39
50674 Cologne Germany
Phone: 0221 39760905

#205
El Allioli
Cuisines: Tapas Bar, Spanish
Average price: Modest
Area: Südstadt
Address: Lothringer Str. 1
50677 Cologne Germany
Phone: 0221 9320120

#206
Oishi
Cuisines: Sushi Bar, Japanese
Average price: Modest
Area: Bayenthal
Address: Bonnerstr. 229 A
50968 Cologne Germany
Phone: 0221 39899453

#207
PigBull BBQ
Cuisines: Fast Food, Barbeque
Average price: Inexpensive
Area: Belgisches Viertel
Address: Aachener Str. 51
50674 Cologne Germany
Phone: 0221 123999

#208
MASSIMO
Cuisines: Italian
Average price: Modest
Area: Südstadt
Address: Alteburger Str. 41
50678 Cologne Germany
Phone: 0221 3489601

#209
Funkhaus
Cuisines: Bar, Cafe, Mediterranean
Average price: Modest
Area: Martinsviertel
Address: Wallrafplatz 5
50667 Cologne Germany
Phone: 0221 955645424

#210
Nikko
Cuisines: Japanese
Average price: Expensive
Area: Lindenthal
Address: Dürener Str. 89
50931 Cologne Germany
Phone: 0221 4000094

#211
Restaurant Zur Tant
Cuisines: German
Average price: Expensive
Area: Langel
Address: Rheinbergstr. 49
51143 Cologne Germany
Phone: 02203 81883

#212
Halet Al Sham
Cuisines: Arabian
Average price: Inexpensive
Area: Martinsviertel
Address: An Sankt Agatha 33-35
50667 Cologne Germany
Phone: 0221 13067336

#213
Sushi Ninja
Cuisines: Sushi Bar, Japanese
Average price: Modest
Area: Sülz
Address: Lindenthalgürtel 2
50935 Cologne Germany
Phone: 0221 4745444

#214
Bibimbab
Cuisines: Korean
Average price: Inexpensive
Area: Kwatier Latäng
Address: Zülpicher Platz 2
50674 Cologne Germany
Phone: 0221 16868622

#215
Alanya Firini
Cuisines: Kebab, Bakery, Falafel
Average price: Inexpensive
Area: Ehrenfeld
Address: Subbelrather Str. 240
50825 Cologne Germany
Phone: 0221 551993

#216
Essers Gasthaus
Cuisines: German, Austrian
Average price: Expensive
Area: Neuehrenfeld
Address: Ottostr. 72
50823 Cologne Germany
Phone: 0221 425954

#217
Indian Curry Basmati House
Cuisines: Indian
Average price: Modest
Area: Severinsviertel
Address: Severinstr. 53
50678 Cologne Germany
Phone: 0221 313128

#218
Saigon Phô
Cuisines: Vietnamese
Average price: Modest
Area: Sülz
Address: Berrenrather Str. 359
50937 Cologne Germany
Phone: 0221 447750

#219
Mataim
Cuisines: Falafel, Breakfast & Brunch
Average price: Modest
Area: Nippes
Address: Neusser Str. 339
50733 Cologne Germany
Phone: 0221 30146691

#220
Lieblings
Cuisines: Cafe, Tapas/Small Plates
Average price: Modest
Area: Sülz
Address: Zülpicher Str. 275
50937 Cologne Germany
Phone: 0221 94388801

#221
De Luxe Pommes
Cuisines: Food Stand
Average price: Inexpensive
Area: Martinsviertel
Address: Schildergasse 54
50667 Cologne Germany
Phone: 0221 13068761

#222
Meister Bock
Cuisines: Food Stand
Average price: Inexpensive
Area: Gereonsviertel
Address: Trankgasse 11
50667 Cologne Germany
Phone: 0221 4735715

#223
Restaurant Heckmanns
Cuisines: French, Mediterranean, German
Average price: Expensive
Area: Sülz
Address: Sülzburgstr. 104 - 106
50937 Cologne Germany
Phone: 0221 94080833

#224
Bunte Burger
Cuisines: Vegan, Burgers
Average price: Modest
Area: Ehrenfeld
Address: Hospeltstr. 1
50825 Cologne Germany
Phone: 0221 59556088

#225
Cafe Casablanca
Cuisines: Cafe, Bakery
Average price: Inexpensive
Area: Humboldt/Gremberg
Address: Taunusstr. 1
51105 Cologne Germany
Phone: 0221 16868578

#226
Gruber's Restaurant
Cuisines: Austrian
Average price: Expensive
Area: Agnesviertel
Address: Clever Str. 32
50668 Cologne Germany
Phone: 0221 7202670

#227
Rheinterrassen
Cuisines: Beer Garden, Venues & Event
Spaces, International
Average price: Expensive
Area: Deutz
Address: Rheinparkweg 1
50679 Cologne Germany
Phone: 0221 6500430

#228
Thai Imbiss
Cuisines: Thai
Average price: Inexpensive
Area: Eigelstein
Address: Eigelstein 114
50668 Cologne Germany
Phone: 0221 16842276

#229
Metzgerei Schmitz
Cuisines: Bistro
Average price: Modest
Area: Belgisches Viertel
Address: Aachenerstr. 30
50674 Cologne Germany
Phone: 0221 1395577

#230
Tomatoes
Cuisines: Pizza, Italian
Average price: Modest
Area: Südstadt
Address: Mainzer Str. 18
50678 Cologne Germany
Phone: 0221 315501

#231
Asien Shop
Cuisines: Asian Fusion
Average price: Inexpensive
Area: Apostelnviertel
Address: Albertusstr. 7
50667 Cologne Germany
Phone: 0221 2574803

#232
Da Luigi
Cuisines: Italian
Average price: Modest
Area: Apostelnviertel
Address: Friesenwall 54
50672 Cologne Germany
Phone: 0163 4275234

#233
Al-Salam
Cuisines: Oriental, Cocktail Bar
Average price: Expensive
Area: Mauritiusviertel
Address: Hohenstaufenring 22
50674 Cologne Germany
Phone: 0221 216713

#234
Menz Burger
Cuisines: Burgers
Average price: Modest
Area: Agnesviertel
Address: Krefelder Str. 12
50670 Cologne Germany
Phone: 0221 72029588

#235
Gilden Brauhaus
Cuisines: Rhinelandian, Gastropub
Average price: Modest
Area: Mülheim
Address: Clevischer Ring 121
51063 Cologne Germany
Phone: 0221 6406339

#236
Restaurant Lannathai
Cuisines: Thai
Average price: Modest
Area: Braunsfeld
Address: Aachener Str. 493
50933 Cologne Germany
Phone: 0221 45341856

#237
Sakura
Cuisines: Japanese, Sushi Bar
Average price: Modest
Area: Sülz
Address: Berrenrather Str. 266
50939 Cologne Germany
Phone: 0221 3201918

#238
La Montanara
Cuisines: Italian
Average price: Modest
Area: Belgisches Viertel
Address: Venloer Str. 8 -10
50672 Cologne Germany
Phone: 0221 5108930

#239
Büyük Harran Doy Doy
Cuisines: Turkish, Kebab
Average price: Modest
Area: Mülheim
Address: Keupstr. 40
51063 Cologne Germany
Phone: 0221 9224347

#240
Pizzeria Rialto
Cuisines: Pizza, Indian
Average price: Inexpensive
Area: Mülheim
Address: Dünnwalder Str. 49
51063 Cologne Germany
Phone: 0221 6406916

#241
Café Rico
Cuisines: Breakfast & Brunch, Bar, Cafe
Average price: Modest
Area: Apostelnviertel
Address: Mittelstr. 31-33
50672 Cologne Germany
Phone: 0221 2405364

#242
Kunstbruder
Cuisines: Cafe, Bar
Average price: Modest
Area: Belgisches Viertel
Address: Händelstr. 51
50674 Cologne Germany
Phone: 0221 22200146

#243
Tasty India
Cuisines: Indian
Average price: Modest
Area: Sülz
Address: Zülpicher Str. 251
50937 Cologne Germany
Phone: 0221 2978387

#244
Haus Müller
Cuisines: European, Bar
Average price: Modest
Area: Severinsviertel
Address: Achterstr. 2
50678 Cologne Germany
Phone: 0221 9321086

#245
Zippiri
Cuisines: Italian, Delicatessen
Average price: Modest
Area: Agnesviertel
Address: Riehler Str. 73
50668 Cologne Germany
Phone: 0221 92299584

#246
Spitz
Cuisines: German
Average price: Modest
Area: Apostelnviertel
Address: Pfeilstr. 31-35
50672 Cologne Germany
Phone: 0221 16909848

#247
Ristorante Alfredo
Cuisines: Italian
Average price: Exclusive
Area: Martinsviertel
Address: Tunisstr. 3
50667 Cologne Germany
Phone: 0221 2577380

#248
Reissdorf am Hahnentor
Cuisines: German
Average price: Modest
Area: Apostelnviertel
Address: Hahnenstr. 24
50667 Cologne Germany
Phone: 0221 2774384

#249
Asiatisches Restaurant Ban Thai
Cuisines: Asian Fusion
Average price: Modest
Area: Bayenthal
Address: Bonner Str. 289
50968 Cologne Germany
Phone: 0221 36798594

#250
Portobello
Cuisines: Pizza, Italian
Average price: Modest
Area: Sülz
Address: Sülzburgstr. 171
50937 Cologne Germany
Phone: 0221 421966

#251
Zur alten Post
Cuisines: Beer Garden, Rhinelandian
Average price: Expensive
Area: Dellbrück
Address: Bergisch Gladbacher Str. 1124
51069 Cologne Germany
Phone: 0221 6639467

#252
Hernando Cortez
Cuisines: Cafe, Chocolatiers & Shop
Average price: Expensive
Area: Neumarkt Viertel
Address: Gertrudenstr. 23
50667 Cologne Germany
Phone: 0221 27250570

#253
Il Valentino
Cuisines: Italian, Pizza
Average price: Inexpensive
Area: Martinsviertel
Address: Herzogstr. 14
50667 Cologne Germany
Phone: 0221 25084909

#254
Osman30
Cuisines: Venues & Event Spaces, European
Average price: Expensive
Area: Mediapark
Address: Im Mediapark 8
50670 Cologne Germany
Phone: 0221 50052080

#255
Restaurant Slavia
Cuisines: Mediterranean,
Serbo Croatian, German
Average price: Modest
Area: Martinsviertel
Address: Am Bollwerk 7
50667 Cologne Germany
Phone: 0221 2580716

#256
Pepe - Restaurant & Bar
Cuisines: Bar, Mediterranean
Average price: Modest
Area: Belgisches Viertel
Address: Antwerpener Str. 63
50672 Cologne Germany
Phone: 0221 5101414

#257
L'Osteria
Cuisines: Italian, Pizza
Average price: Modest
Area: Mauritiusviertel
Address: Hahnenstr. 37
50667 Cologne Germany
Phone: 0221 33108383

#258
kitchenette
Cuisines: Salad, Cafe
Average price: Inexpensive
Area: Belgisches Viertel
Address: Gladbacher Str. 15
50672 Cologne Germany
Phone: 0221 6606603

#259
La Diffèrence
Cuisines: French, Mediterranean, Bistro
Average price: Modest
Area: Agnesviertel
Address: Hansaring 131
50670 Cologne Germany
Phone: 0221 731756

#260
Trattoria Palermo da Salvatore
Cuisines: Italian
Average price: Inexpensive
Area: Severinsviertel
Address: Severinstr. 151
50678 Cologne Germany
Phone: 0221 329131

#261
Feuerstein's
Cuisines: Burgers, Barbeque
Average price: Modest
Area: Bickendorf
Address: Venloer Str. 601
50827 Cologne Germany
Phone: 0221 99558039

#262
Oxin
Cuisines: Arabian
Average price: Modest
Area: Südstadt
Address: Alteburger Str. 35
50678 Cologne Germany
Phone: 0221 9322464

#263
Imperial Ristorante
Cuisines: Italian, Steakhouse, Pizza
Average price: Modest
Area: Eil
Address: Frankfurter Str. 641
51145 Cologne Germany
Phone: 02203 9171966

#264
Geißbockheim
Cuisines: German
Average price: Modest
Area: Sülz
Address: Franz-Kremer-Allee 1-3
50937 Cologne Germany
Phone: 0221 716166470

#265
La Esquina
Cuisines: Tapas Bar
Average price: Modest
Area: Severinsviertel
Address: Severinstr. 41
50678 Cologne Germany
Phone: 0221 8696840

#266
Via Bene
Cuisines: Italian
Average price: Expensive
Area: Apostelnviertel
Address: Benesisstr. 60-62
50672 Cologne Germany
Phone: 0221 2578166

#267
China Imbiss Wei Wei
Cuisines: Chinese
Average price: Inexpensive
Area: Zollstock
Address: Gottesweg 29
50969 Cologne Germany
Phone: 0221 3604975

#268
Doy Doy Palast
Cuisines: Turkish
Average price: Modest
Area: Eigelstein
Address: Weidengasse 71-73
50668 Cologne Germany
Phone: 0221 27075744

#269
Peperino
Cuisines: Italian
Average price: Modest
Area: Südstadt
Address: Chlodwigplatz 5
50678 Cologne Germany
Phone: 0221 3679686

#270
Nudel Mafia
Cuisines: Italian, Food Stand
Average price: Modest
Area: Agnesviertel
Address: Neusser Str. 24
50670 Cologne Germany
Phone: 0221 16927733

#271
Restaurant Carls
Cuisines: German
Average price: Expensive
Area: Neuehrenfeld
Address: Eichendorffstr. 25
50823 Cologne Germany
Phone: 0221 58986656

#272
Haus Unkelbach
Cuisines: Dive Bar, German
Average price: Modest
Area: Klettenberg
Address: Luxemburger Str. 260
50937 Cologne Germany
Phone: 0221 414184

#273
New Konfuzius
Cuisines: Chinese
Average price: Modest
Area: Eigelstein
Address: Thürmchenswall 3
50668 Cologne Germany
Phone: 0221 1392937

#274
WIPPN'BK
Cuisines: Breakfast & Brunch, European
Average price: Modest
Area: Severinsviertel
Address: Ubierring 35
50678 Cologne Germany
Phone: 0221 326133

#275
Sophias Restaurant
Cuisines: German, Greek
Average price: Expensive
Area: Klettenberg
Address: Luxemburger Str. 289
50939 Cologne Germany
Phone: 0221 16948824

#276
Cafe Alsen
Cuisines: Cafe, Patisserie/Cake Shop
Average price: Inexpensive
Area: Riehl
Address: Stammheimer Str. 102
50735 Cologne Germany
Phone: 0221 97757740

#277
Daitokai
Cuisines: Japanese, Sushi Bar
Average price: Expensive
Area: Gereonsviertel
Address: Kattenbug 2
50667 Cologne Germany
Phone: 0221 120048

#278
Tasso's Grill
Cuisines: Greek
Average price: Inexpensive
Area: Weiden
Address: Aachener Str. 1283
50859 Cologne Germany
Phone: 02234 70639

#279
Pane e vino
Cuisines: Italian
Average price: Modest
Area: Volksgartenviertel
Address: Eifelstr. 18
50677 Cologne Germany
Phone: 0221 9311311

#280
Tang Wang Köln
Cuisines: Chinese
Average price: Modest
Area: Kunibertsviertel
Address: Maximinenstr. 4
50668 Cologne Germany
Phone: 0221 82956288

#281
Bier-Esel
Cuisines: Seafood, German
Average price: Modest
Area: Neumarkt Viertel
Address: Breite Str. 114
50667 Cologne Germany
Phone: 0221 2576090

#282
Akira
Cuisines: Sushi Bar, Japanese
Average price: Modest
Area: Gereonsviertel
Address: Hildeboldplatz 1
50672 Cologne Germany
Phone: 0221 33766667

#283
Mitica Italia
Cuisines: Italian
Average price: Modest
Area: Nippes
Address: Scharnhorststr. 8
50733 Cologne Germany
Phone: 0221 -765795

#284
Tapas y Tapas
Cuisines: Tapas Bar
Average price: Modest
Area: Gereonsviertel
Address: Friesenwall 81
50672 Cologne Germany
Phone: 0221 94646514

#285
Café Braun
Cuisines: Cafe, Patisserie/Cake Shop
Average price: Modest
Area: Rathenauviertel
Address: Lindenstr. 97
50674 Cologne Germany
Phone: 0221 214729

#286
Restaurant Willomitzer
Cuisines: German, Mediterranean
Average price: Modest
Area: Mülheim
Address: Mülheimer Freiheit 2-4
51063 Cologne Germany
Phone: 0221 16839317

#287
Sant' Angelo
Cuisines: Italian, Bar
Average price: Inexpensive
Area: Agnesviertel
Address: Aquinostr. 1 A
50670 Cologne Germany
Phone: 0221 731653

#288
Lai Thai 2 Restaurant
Cuisines: Thai, Vegetarian
Average price: Modest
Area: Georgsviertel
Address: Blaubach 18
50676 Cologne Germany
Phone: 0221 8016060

#289
Ehrenfelder Zeitgeist
Cuisines: German
Average price: Inexpensive
Area: Ehrenfeld
Address: Stammstr. 2 a
50823 Cologne Germany
Phone: 0221 523414

#290
Joseph's
Cuisines: German, Austrian, European
Average price: Expensive
Area: Südstadt
Address: Agrippinawerft 22
50678 Cologne Germany
Phone: 0221 16917300

#291
Kyoto
Cuisines: Japanese, Sushi Bar, Asian Fusion
Average price: Expensive
Area: Belgisches Viertel
Address: Brüsseler Str. 12
50674 Cologne Germany
Phone: 0221 2404626

#292
Maria Eetcafe
Cuisines: Belgian
Average price: Modest
Area: Belgisches Viertel
Address: Hans-Böckler-Platz 1-3
50672 Cologne Germany
Phone: 0221 94657878

#293
Pizzeria La Rustica
Cuisines: Italian
Average price: Inexpensive
Area: Kalk
Address: Kalker Hauptstr. 66
51103 Cologne Germany
Phone: 0221 98949035

#294
Pizzeria Palazzo Ristorante
Cuisines: Pizza
Average price: Inexpensive
Area: Mülheim
Address: Clevischer Ring 3
51065 Cologne Germany
Phone: 0221 6201989

#295

Cuisines: Steakhouse, Argentine
Average price: Modest
Area: Leverkusen
Address: Alkenrather Str 6
51377 Leverkusen Germany
Phone: 0214 2029955

#296
Asia Gourmet Hakka
Cuisines: Chinese
Average price: Modest
Area: Braunsfeld
Address: Aachener Str. 431
50933 Cologne Germany
Phone: 0221 42348758

#297
Öz Harran Doy Doy
Cuisines: Food Stand, Kebab, Turkish
Average price: Modest
Area: Eigelstein
Address: Weidengasse 28-34
50668 Cologne Germany
Phone: 0221 1307394

#298
The Shepler's
Cuisines: American, Sports Bar
Average price: Modest
Area: Ehrenfeld
Address: Subbelrather Str. 269
50825 Cologne Germany
Phone: 0221 16924349

#299
Acht
Cuisines: European
Average price: Expensive
Area: Belgisches Viertel
Address: Spichernstr. 10
50672 Cologne Germany
Phone: 0221 16818408

#300
Saana
Cuisines: Oriental
Average price: Inexpensive
Area: Kalk
Address: Kalker Hauptstr. 105
51103 Cologne Germany
Phone: 0221 47178994

#301
Distinto
Cuisines: Italian
Average price: Expensive
Area: Junkersdorf
Address: Kirchweg 8
50858 Cologne Germany
Phone: 0221 50067999

#302
Pizzeria Mimmo u. Santo
Cuisines: Pizza, Italian
Average price: Modest
Area: Nippes
Address: Neusser Str. 336
50733 Cologne Germany
Phone: 0221 763746

#303
Teatro
Cuisines: Italian
Average price: Expensive
Area: Südstadt
Address: Zugweg 1
50677 Cologne Germany
Phone: 0221 80158020

#304
Haus Zeyen
Cuisines: Rhinelandian, Steakhouse
Average price: Inexpensive
Area: Deutz
Address: Neuhöfferstr. 27-29
50679 Cologne Germany
Phone: 0221 29755327

#305
Shokudo
Cuisines: Sushi Bar, Ramen
Average price: Modest
Area: Belgisches Viertel
Address: Lützowstr. 41
50674 Cologne Germany
Phone: 0221 2760188

#306
Ristorante Pinocchio
Cuisines: Italian, Pizza
Average price: Modest
Area: Martinsviertel
Address: Salzgasse 11
50667 Cologne Germany
Phone: 0221 2577918

#307
Athen's
Cuisines: Greek, Wine Bar
Average price: Modest
Area: Georgsviertel
Address: Heumarkt 2 - 4
50667 Cologne Germany
Phone: 0221 246360

#308
Manuela
Cuisines: Tapas Bar
Average price: Modest
Area: Kwatier Latäng
Address: Mozartstr. 9
50674 Cologne Germany
Phone: 0221 2224864

#309
Little India
Cuisines: Indian
Average price: Inexpensive
Area: Rathenauviertel
Address: Luxemburger Str. 42
50674 Cologne Germany
Phone: 0221 2618817

#310
Ginti
Cuisines: Indian, Caterers
Average price: Modest
Area: Belgisches Viertel
Address: Händelstr. 33
50674 Cologne Germany
Phone: 0221 99029466

#311
Etrusca Ristorante
Cuisines: Italian
Average price: Expensive
Area: Rathenauviertel
Address: Zülpicher Str. 27
50674 Cologne Germany
Phone: 0221 2403900

#312
Thai Basilikum
Cuisines: Thai
Average price: Inexpensive
Area: Cäcilienviertel
Address: Fleischmengergasse 59
50676 Cologne Germany
Phone: 0221 93299858

#313
Fasika
Cuisines: African, Ethiopian
Average price: Modest
Area: Volksgartenviertel
Address: Luxemburger Str. 17
50674 Cologne Germany
Phone: 0221 4204891

#314
Fuji
Cuisines: Japanese
Average price: Modest
Area: Ehrenfeld
Address: Venloer Str. 242
50823 Cologne Germany
Phone: 0221 16835301

#315
Nagoya
Cuisines: Sushi Bar
Average price: Modest
Area: Gereonsviertel
Address: Hohenzollernring 94
50672 Cologne Germany
Phone: 0221 16823299

#316
Ferkulum
Cuisines: Food Stand
Average price: Modest
Area: Rathenauviertel
Address: Zülpicher Str. 37
50674 Cologne Germany
Phone: 0221 213796

#317
TörtchenTörtchen
Cuisines: Desserts, Cafe
Average price: Exclusive
Area: Nippes
Address: Neusser Str. 325
50733 Cologne Germany
Phone: 0221 17050844

#318
Carlos
Cuisines: Cuban, Spanish
Average price: Modest
Area: Lindenthal
Address: Dürener Str. 152
50931 Cologne Germany
Phone: 0221 9907688

#319
Gasthaus im 1/4
Cuisines: German
Average price: Modest
Area: Nippes
Address: Holbeinstr. 35
50733 Cologne Germany
Phone: 0221 16824422

#320
Hallmackenreuther
Cuisines: International, Cafe, Bar
Average price: Modest
Area: Belgisches Viertel
Address: Brüsseler Platz 9
50674 Cologne Germany
Phone: 0221 517970

#321
L' Assagio
Cuisines: Italian
Average price: Expensive
Area: Marienburg
Address: Bonner Str. 471
50968 Cologne Germany
Phone: 0221 2807854

#322
Restaurant Latio
Cuisines: Italian
Average price: Modest
Area: Südstadt
Address: Vorgebirgstr. 1
50677 Cologne Germany
Phone: 0221 8016007

#323
Salädchen Kölle
Cuisines: Salad
Average price: Modest
Area: Gereonsviertel
Address: Kaiser-Wilhelm-Ring 40
50672 Cologne Germany
Phone: 0221 29895026

#324
Hans Im Glück
Cuisines: Burgers, Cocktail Bar
Average price: Modest
Area: Apostelnviertel
Address: Hohenzollernring 38 - 40
50672 Cologne Germany
Phone: 0221 29892163

#325
Namaste
Cuisines: Indian
Average price: Modest
Area: Kunibertsviertel
Address: Domstr. 82
50668 Cologne Germany
Phone: 0221 92278908

#326
Restaurant Diogenis
Cuisines: Greek
Average price: Modest
Area: Agnesviertel
Address: Sudermanplatz 7
50670 Cologne Germany
Phone: 0221 729231

#327
Einheit 15
Cuisines: European
Average price: Modest
Area: Nippes
Address: Einheitstr. 15
50733 Cologne Germany
Phone: 0221 7882627

#328
maiBeck
Cuisines: European
Average price: Expensive
Area: Martinsviertel
Address: Am Frankenturm 5
50667 Cologne Germany
Phone: 0221 96267300

#329
Hotzenplotz
Cuisines: German, Gastropub
Average price: Modest
Area: Neuehrenfeld
Address: Chamissostr. 2
50825 Cologne Germany
Phone: 0221 2822727

#330
Sushi Nara
Cuisines: Sushi Bar
Average price: Modest
Area: Gereonsviertel
Address: Friesenstr. 70
50670 Cologne Germany
Phone: 0221 120190

#331
Vinoteca Da Rino
Cuisines: Italian
Average price: Inexpensive
Area: Martinsviertel
Address: Kolumbastr. 5
50667 Cologne Germany
Phone: 0221 2575647

#332
Vapiano
Cuisines: Italian, Fast Food, Pizza
Average price: Modest
Area: Deutz
Address: Constantinstr. 87-89
50679 Cologne Germany
Phone: 0221 8008833

#333
CurryCologne
Cuisines: Curry Sausage
Average price: Modest
Area: Belgisches Viertel
Address: Brabanter Str. 42
50672 Cologne Germany
Phone: 0221 5894556

#334
Meta
Cuisines: International, Cafe, Cocktail Bar
Average price: Expensive
Area: Poll
Address: Siegburger Str. 385 - 387
51105 Cologne Germany
Phone: 0221 29997067

#335
Yummy Town
Cuisines: Chinese, Mongolian, Sushi Bar
Average price: Modest
Area: Zollstock
Address: Höninger Weg 218 B
50969 Cologne Germany
Phone: 0221 39804087

#336
Adolph's Gasthaus
Cuisines: German, Bakery
Average price: Modest
Area: Longerich
Address: Rüdellstr. 1
50737 Cologne Germany
Phone: 0221 974515-0

#337
Restaurant Keule
Cuisines: German
Average price: Modest
Area: Martinsviertel
Address: Heumarkt 56 - 58
50667 Cologne Germany
Phone: 0221 2581159

#338
Gertrudenhof
Cuisines: German
Average price: Modest
Area: Neumarkt Viertel
Address: Apostelnstr. 2 A
50667 Cologne Germany
Phone: 0221 54814143

#339
Alt Melaten
Cuisines: Serbo Croatian
Average price: Modest
Area: Lindenthal
Address: Aachener Str. 321
50931 Cologne Germany
Phone: 0221 405651

#340
Südstadt Burger
Cuisines: Burgers
Average price: Modest
Area: Südstadt
Address: Merowingerstr. 29
50677 Cologne Germany
Phone: 0221 22200216

#341
Mersin Tantuni & Kebap Salonu
Cuisines: Turkish, Kebab
Average price: Inexpensive
Area: Südstadt
Address: Merowingerstr. 3
50677 Cologne Germany
Phone: 0221 4767503

#342
Salon Schmitz
Cuisines: Bar, Cafe
Average price: Modest
Area: Belgisches Viertel
Address: Aachener Str. 28
50674 Cologne Germany
Phone: 0221 1395577

#343
Zum alten Brauhaus
Cuisines: German
Average price: Modest
Area: Severinsviertel
Address: Severinstr. 51
50678 Cologne Germany
Phone: 0221 60608780

#344
Pizza-Pazza
Cuisines: Pizza
Average price: Inexpensive
Area: Rathenauviertel
Address: Hochstadenstr. 35
50674 Cologne Germany
Phone: 0221 3108733

#345
La Guitarra
Cuisines: Spanish, Tapas Bar
Average price: Modest
Area: Südstadt
Address: Alteburger Str. 20
50678 Cologne Germany
Phone: 0221 319297

#346
Pinocchio Imbiss Pizzeria
Cuisines: Italian, Fast Food, Pizza
Average price: Inexpensive
Area: Poll
Address: Salmstr. 1
51105 Cologne Germany
Phone: 0221 16832075

#347
Riphahn
Cuisines: French, German, Cafe
Average price: Modest
Area: Apostelnviertel
Address: Apostelnkloster 2
50672 Cologne Germany
Phone: 0221 99874577

#348
Café Franck
Cuisines: Lounges, Cafe
Average price: Modest
Area: Neuehrenfeld
Address: Eichendorffstr. 30
50825 Cologne Germany
Phone: 0221 7167210

#349
3h's burger & chicken
Cuisines: Burgers
Average price: Modest
Area: Bayenthal
Address: Koblenzer Str. 1-9
50968 Cologne Germany
Phone: 0221 30193025

#350
Rhodos Grill
Cuisines: Greek, Food Stand, Pizza
Average price: Modest
Area: Rodenkirchen
Address: Weißer Str. 43
50996 Cologne Germany
Phone: 0221 351111

#351
Indian Masala
Cuisines: Indian
Average price: Inexpensive
Area: Deutz
Address: Graf-Geßler-Str. 2
50679 Cologne Germany
Phone: 0221 82959990

#352
Kittichai Köln
Cuisines: Thai, Bar, Sushi Bar
Average price: Modest
Area: Martinsviertel
Address: Alter Markt 36-42
50667 Cologne Germany
Phone: 0221 25099551

#353
Cafe Laura
Cuisines: Coffee & Tea, Cafe
Average price: Modest
Area: Georgsviertel
Address: Hohe Pforte 29
50676 Cologne Germany
Phone: 0221 29853583

#354
Sam's Mexican Döner
Cuisines: Kebab, Halal, Fast Food
Average price: Modest
Area: Mülheim
Address: Genovevastr. 2
51065 Cologne Germany
Phone: 0178 7232186

#355
Pizza Azzurro
Cuisines: Pizza
Average price: Inexpensive
Area: Sülz
Address: Berrenrather Str. 346
50937 Cologne Germany
Phone: 0221 2900646

#356
Schlüters in Weidenpesch
Cuisines: International
Average price: Modest
Area: Weidenpesch
Address: Neusser Str. 494
50737 Cologne Germany
Phone: 0221 16879507

#357
Paparazzi
Cuisines: Bar, Italian
Average price: Expensive
Area: Deutz
Address: Messe-Kreisel 3
50679 Cologne Germany
Phone: 0221 277203466

#358
Lebanon Vitamin
Cuisines: Food Stand, Lebanese, Halal
Average price: Inexpensive
Area: Rathenauviertel
Address: Zülpicher Str. 38-40
50674 Cologne Germany
Phone: 0221 2402700

#359
Bellavista
Cuisines: Italian
Average price: Modest
Area: Sülz
Address: Sülzburgstr. 200
50937 Cologne Germany
Phone: 0221 415654

#360
Il Gelato di Ferigo
Cuisines: Ice Cream & Frozen Yogurt, Cafe
Average price: Expensive
Area: Bayenthal
Address: Goltsteinstr. 32
50968 Cologne Germany
Phone: 0221 341888

#361
Weinstube Bacchus
Cuisines: Wine Bar, German
Average price: Modest
Area: Rathenauviertel
Address: Rathenauplatz 17
50674 Cologne Germany
Phone: 0221 217986

#362
Mamounia Bistro
Cuisines: Moroccan, Coffee & Tea
Average price: Modest
Area: Severinsviertel
Address: Severinstr. 90
50678 Cologne Germany
Phone: 0172 9733399

#363
Gea
Cuisines: Ice Cream & Frozen Yogurt, Cafe
Average price: Inexpensive
Area: Severinsviertel
Address: Severinstr. 124
50678 Cologne Germany
Phone: 0221 99558441

#364
Arnolds Kartöffelchen
Cuisines: German, Vegetarian,
Tapas/Small Plates
Average price: Expensive
Area: Südstadt
Address: Darmstädter Str. 9
50678 Cologne Germany
Phone: 0221 16912747

#365
Haus Töller
Cuisines: German
Average price: Modest
Area: Mauritiusviertel
Address: Weyerstr. 96
50676 Cologne Germany
Phone: 0221 2589316

#366
Kaffeebud Ehrenfeld
Cuisines: Cafe, Breakfast & Brunch
Average price: Modest
Area: Ehrenfeld
Address: Glasstr. 62
50823 Cologne Germany
Phone: 0174 2523233

#367
Trattoria Salento
Cuisines: Italian
Average price: Expensive
Area: Neuehrenfeld
Address: Schadowstr. 55
50823 Cologne Germany
Phone: 0221 5506828

#368
Pizzeria San Remo
Cuisines: Pizza, Italian
Average price: Modest
Area: Eigelstein
Address: Weidengasse 76
50668 Cologne Germany
Phone: 0221 121272

#369
The Bird
Cuisines: Steakhouse, Burgers
Average price: Modest
Area: Belgisches Viertel
Address: Aachener Str. 9
50674 Cologne Germany
Phone: 0176 83369684

#370
Gyrosland
Cuisines: Food Stand
Average price: Inexpensive
Area: Ehrenfeld
Address: Vogelsanger Str. 106 - 108
50823 Cologne Germany
Phone: 0221 16991261

#371
Grill-Stübchen
Cuisines: Fast Food
Average price: Expensive
Area: Buchforst
Address: Heidelberger Str. 23
51065 Cologne Germany
Phone: 0221 621406

#372
Il Valentino
Cuisines: Italian
Average price: Modest
Area: Rondorf
Address: Rodenkirchener Str. 61
50997 Cologne Germany
Phone: 02233 712313

#373
Restaurant Dalmacija
Cuisines: Serbo Croatian
Average price: Inexpensive
Area: Georgsviertel
Address: Agrippastr 6
50676 Cologne Germany
Phone: 0221 2405445

#374
Bangkok Thai-Restaurant
Cuisines: Thai, Cocktail Bar
Average price: Modest
Area: Rathenauviertel
Address: Lindenstr. 81
50674 Cologne Germany
Phone: 0221 80162378

#375
Café Fleur
Cuisines: Breakfast & Brunch, Cafe
Average price: Modest
Area: Belgisches Viertel
Address: Lindenstr. 10
50674 Cologne Germany
Phone: 0221 244897

#376
Café-Restaurant Stadtgarten
Cuisines: Beer Garden, Cafe
Average price: Modest
Area: Belgisches Viertel
Address: Venloer Str. 40
50672 Cologne Germany
Phone: 0221 9529940

#377
Hyatt Biergarten
Cuisines: Beer Garden
Average price: Modest
Area: Deutz
Address: Hyatt Regency Köln
50679 Cologne Germany
Phone: 0221 82811760

#378
Brauhaus Quetsch
Cuisines: Gastropub, Rhinelandian
Average price: Modest
Area: Rodenkirchen
Address: Hauptstr. 7
50996 Cologne Germany
Phone: 0221 26036803

#379
Kölsche Art
Cuisines: German
Average price: Expensive
Area: Braunsfeld
Address: Aachener Str. 607
50933 Cologne Germany
Phone: 0221 5008034

#380
Linos
Cuisines: Italian, Tapas/Small Plates
Average price: Expensive
Area: Rodenkirchen
Address: Kirchstr. 2
50996 Cologne Germany
Phone: 0221 39809889

#381
Der Walfisch
Cuisines: Brewery, Gastropub
Average price: Modest
Area: Martinsviertel
Address: Salzgasse 13
50667 Cologne Germany
Phone: 0221 2577879

#382
Warung Bayu
Cuisines: Indonesian
Average price: Modest
Area: Belgisches Viertel
Address: Brabanter Str. 5
50674 Cologne Germany
Phone: 0221 5894366

#383
Leo Am Eigelsteintor
Cuisines: Cafe
Average price: Modest
Area: Eigelstein
Address: Lübecker Str. 2
50668 Cologne Germany
Phone: 0221 1206206

#384
Café Central
Cuisines: Cafe, German, Whiskey Bar
Average price: Modest
Area: Belgisches Viertel
Address: Jülicher Str. 1
50674 Cologne Germany
Phone: 0221 2071520

#385
Wagenhalle Comedia
Cuisines: German, French
Average price: Expensive
Area: Südstadt
Address: Vondelstr. 4-8
50677 Cologne Germany
Phone: 0221 35558910

#386
Grande il Piatto
Cuisines: Pizza, Italian
Average price: Modest
Area: Belgisches Viertel
Address: Flandrische Str. 2
50674 Cologne Germany
Phone: 0221 16898418

#387
Bon Frit
Cuisines: Burgers, Belgian
Average price: Modest
Area: Sülz
Address: Palanterstr. 12 A
50937 Cologne Germany
Phone: 0221 79007186

#388
Biergarten Am Rathenauplatz
Cuisines: Beer Garden
Average price: Modest
Area: Rathenauviertel
Address: Rathenauplatz 30
50674 Cologne Germany
Phone: 0221 8017349

#389
Hot POinT
Cuisines: Chinese
Average price: Modest
Area: Pantaleonsviertel
Address: Salierring 44
50667 Cologne Germany
Phone: 0221 242400

#390
Gasthaus zur Linde
Cuisines: Mediterranean, German
Average price: Modest
Area: Agnesviertel
Address: Balthasarstr. 2
50670 Cologne Germany
Phone: 0221 99207654

#391
Pizzeria da Enzo
Cuisines: Pizza, Italian
Average price: Modest
Area: Longerich
Address: Longericher Hauptstr. 72
50739 Cologne Germany
Phone: 0221 5994296

#392
Melange Orange
Cuisines: Cafe
Average price: Modest
Area: Sülz
Address: Sülzburgstr. 23
50937 Cologne Germany
Phone: 02234 2519194

#393
Trattoria Silvano
Cuisines: Italian
Average price: Modest
Area: Martinsviertel
Address: Komödienstr 43
50667 Cologne Germany
Phone: 0221 2704989

#394
Haus Schnackertz
Cuisines: German
Average price: Modest
Area: Nippes
Address: Bülowstr. 2
50733 Cologne Germany
Phone: 0221 766839

#395
Papa-Pizza
Cuisines: Italian
Average price: Inexpensive
Area: Zollstock
Address: Höninger Weg 107
50969 Cologne Germany
Phone: 0221 364502

#396
Weinhaus zur alten Schule
Cuisines: Wine Bar, German
Average price: Exclusive
Area: Brück
Address: Olpener Str. 928
51109 Cologne Germany
Phone: 0221 844888

#397
Balthasar im Agnesviertel
Cuisines: Pubs, German
Average price: Modest
Area: Agnesviertel
Address: Neusser Str. 40
50670 Cologne Germany
Phone: 0221 16832185

#398
Pik Thai
Cuisines: Thai
Average price: Modest
Area: Neumarkt Viertel
Address: Wolfsstr. 14
50667 Cologne Germany
Phone: 0221 28066220

#399
Kääzmanns
Cuisines: German
Average price: Modest
Area: Bickendorf
Address: Subbelrather Str. 543
50827 Cologne Germany
Phone: 0221 16897430

#400
Grill Restaurant Zeus
Cuisines: Greek, Fast Food
Average price: Modest
Area: Weidenpesch
Address: Neusser Str. 624
50737 Cologne Germany
Phone: 0221 7406104

#401
Maison Baguette
Cuisines: Baguettes, Creperies
Average price: Modest
Area: Ehrenfeld
Address: Venloer Str. 240
50823 Cologne Germany
Phone: 0221 16867254

#402
Okinii
Cuisines: Sushi Bar, Japanese
Average price: Expensive
Area: Georgsviertel
Address: Blaubach 1
50676 Cologne Germany
Phone: 0221 33178190

#403
Mongo's
Cuisines: Mongolian, Asian Fusion, Buffets
Average price: Expensive
Area: Deutz
Address: Ottoplatz 1
50679 Cologne Germany
Phone: 0221 9893810

#404
Diana
Cuisines: Pizza, Italian
Average price: Modest
Area: Deutz
Address: Deutzer Freiheit 72
50679 Cologne Germany
Phone: 0221 8008793

#405
Asmali Konak
Cuisines: Turkish
Average price: Modest
Area: Mülheim
Address: Keupstr. 44-46
51063 Cologne Germany
Phone: 0221 9385725

#406
Alte Metzgerei
Cuisines: Burgers, Food Stand
Average price: Modest
Area: Dellbrück
Address: Bergisch Gladbacher Str. 974
51069 Cologne Germany
Phone: 0221 58479302

#407
Speisemeister
Cuisines: European
Average price: Inexpensive
Area: Ehrenfeld
Address: Subbelrather Str. 270
50825 Cologne Germany
Phone: 0221 2507762

#408
Saudade
Cuisines: Wine Bar, Portuguese
Average price: Modest
Area: Ehrenfeld
Address: Wahlenstr. 2
50823 Cologne Germany
Phone: 0221 5796476

#409
Nimet Grill
Cuisines: Turkish, Kebab
Average price: Inexpensive
Area: Südstadt
Address: Bonner Str. 18
50677 Cologne Germany
Phone: 0221 3109999

#410
Maifeld
Cuisines: Bistro, Cafe
Average price: Modest
Area: Neuehrenfeld
Address: Simarplatz 10
50825 Cologne Germany
Phone: 0221 5955906

#411
Rim Khong
Cuisines: Thai
Average price: Inexpensive
Area: Südstadt
Address: Elsaßstr. 53
50677 Cologne Germany
Phone: 0221 82823496

#412
Kittichai Köln
Cuisines: Asian Fusion, Cocktail Bar
Average price: Modest
Area: Apostelnviertel
Address: Ehrenstr. 81
50672 Cologne Germany
Phone: 0221 27263840

#413
La Strada
Cuisines: Italian
Average price: Modest
Area: Belgisches Viertel
Address: Hohenzollernring 13
50672 Cologne Germany
Phone: 0221 251865

#414
Caveedel
Cuisines: Cafe, Breakfast & Brunch
Average price: Modest
Area: Belgisches Viertel
Address: Brüsseler Str. 69
50672 Cologne Germany
Phone: 0177 2374368

#415
La Tagliatella
Cuisines: Italian
Average price: Modest
Area: Martinsviertel
Address: Heumarkt 52
50667 Cologne Germany
Phone: 0221 25083028

#416
Westflügel
Cuisines: Breakfast & Brunch,
Mediterranean, Cafe
Average price: Inexpensive
Area: Eigelstein
Address: Weidengasse 56
50668 Cologne Germany
Phone: 0221 92293033

#417
Dürümcü Harran Doy Doy
Cuisines: Kebab
Average price: Modest
Area: Mülheim
Address: Keupstr. 21
51063 Cologne Germany
Phone: 01986 7376

#418
Lütticher
Cuisines: European
Average price: Expensive
Area: Belgisches Viertel
Address: Lütticher Str. 12
50674 Cologne Germany
Phone: 0221 525453

#419
Madame Thy
Cuisines: Vietnamese, Laotian
Average price: Modest
Area: Belgisches Viertel
Address: Brabanter Str. 9
50674 Cologne Germany
Phone: 0221 58938033

#420
Taverne Athos
Cuisines: Greek
Average price: Modest
Area: Agnesviertel
Address: Krefelder Str. 11
50670 Cologne Germany
Phone: 0221 728356

#421
Die Suppenbar
Cuisines: Soup
Average price: Modest
Area: Gereonsviertel
Address: Komödienstr. 99
50667 Cologne Germany
Phone: 0221 9139964

#422
Pizzeria Trattoria Toscana
Cuisines: Pizza, Italian
Average price: Modest
Area: Ehrenfeld
Address: Venloer Str. 440
50825 Cologne Germany
Phone: 0221 5955577

#423
Al-Andalus
Cuisines: Spanish, Steakhouse, Tapas Bar
Average price: Expensive
Area: Belgisches Viertel
Address: Gladbacher Str. 16
50672 Cologne Germany
Phone: 0221 22200830

#424
Em Altertümche
Cuisines: German
Average price: Inexpensive
Area: Eigelstein
Address: Ritterstr. 57
50670 Cologne Germany
Phone: 0221 131434

#425
Damaskus Haus
Cuisines: Arabian, Patisserie/Cake Shop
Average price: Inexpensive
Area: Gereonsviertel
Address: Friesenstr. 77
50670 Cologne Germany
Phone: 0179 4854302

#426
Ouzeria
Cuisines: Tapas Bar, Spanish
Average price: Expensive
Area: Belgisches Viertel
Address: Brüsseler Str. 68
50674 Cologne Germany
Phone: 0221 513998

#427
Woyton
Cuisines: Cafe
Average price: Modest
Area: Neumarkt Viertel
Address: Breite Str. 80-90
50667 Cologne Germany
Phone: 0221 2708680

#428
Evia
Cuisines: Greek, International
Average price: Modest
Area: Merheim
Address: Olpener Str. 494
51109 Cologne Germany
Phone: 0221 893789

#429
Club Astoria
Cuisines: Venues & Event Spaces, European
Average price: Expensive
Area: Lindenthal
Address: Guths-Muths-Weg 3
50933 Cologne Germany
Phone: 0221 9874510

#430
Causas Peru
Cuisines: Peruvian
Average price: Expensive
Area: Ehrenfeld
Address: Venloer Str. 531
50825 Cologne Germany
Phone: 0221 44902886

#431
The Great Berry
Cuisines: Breakfast & Brunch,
Juice Bar & Smoothies, Cafe
Average price: Modest
Area: Belgisches Viertel
Address: Limburger Str. 18
50672 Cologne Germany
Phone: 0221 45580554

#432
Schlechtrimen
Cuisines: Bakery, Cafe,
Patisserie/Cake Shop
Average price: Modest
Area: Kalk
Address: Kalker Hauptstr. 210
51103 Cologne Germany
Phone: 0221 987170

#433
ROCIOS
Cuisines: Seafood, Spanish, Tapas Bar
Average price: Exclusive
Area: Südstadt
Address: Elsaßstr. 30
50677 Cologne Germany
Phone: 0221 16826625

#434
Alter Zollhof
Cuisines: Beer Garden, Gastropub, Mediterranean
Average price: Modest
Area: Zollstock
Address: Herthastr. 64
50969 Cologne Germany
Phone: 0175 4849243

#435
Halli Galli
Cuisines: Parent Cafe
Average price: Modest
Area: Kwatier Latäng
Address: Mozartstr. 39
50674 Cologne Germany
Phone: 0221 60601919

#436
Il Bagutta
Cuisines: Italian
Average price: Expensive
Area: Rathenauviertel
Address: Heinsbergstr. 20 A
50674 Cologne Germany
Phone: 0221 212694

#437
Anno Pomm
Cuisines: German
Average price: Modest
Area: Junkersdorf
Address: Wilhelm-von-Capitaine-Str. 15 - 17
50858 Cologne Germany
Phone: 0221 4849882

#438
épi
Cuisines: Cafe
Average price: Expensive
Area: Agnesviertel
Address: Neusser Str. 32
50670 Cologne Germany
Phone: 0221 37996656

#439
Ristorante Zucchini
Cuisines: Pizza, Italian
Average price: Modest
Area: Mülheim
Address: Graf-Adolf-Str. 60
51065 Cologne Germany
Phone: 0221 614230

#440
Dialog
Cuisines: Greek, Wine Bar
Average price: Inexpensive
Area: Südstadt
Address: Alteburger Str. 26
50678 Cologne Germany
Phone: 0221 327375

#441
Thai Food 2
Cuisines: Thai
Average price: Inexpensive
Area: Apostelnviertel
Address: Friesenwall 24 B
50672 Cologne Germany
Phone: 0221 27799579

#442
Restaurant Altes Fachwerkhaus
Cuisines: International
Average price: Expensive
Area: Sürth
Address: Falderstr. 29
50999 Cologne Germany
Phone: 02236 68716

#443
Ego
Cuisines: Italian
Average price: Expensive
Area: Apostelnviertel
Address: Benesisstr. 57
50672 Cologne Germany
Phone: 0221 9906041

#444
Pizzeria Pinocchio
Cuisines: Pizza, Italian
Average price: Modest
Area: Belgisches Viertel
Address: Gladbacher Str. 39
50672 Cologne Germany
Phone: 0221 526819

#445
Jonny Turista
Cuisines: Bar, Spanish
Average price: Modest
Area: Mauritiusviertel
Address: Mauritiussteinweg 74
50676 Cologne Germany
Phone: 0221 2407055

#446
Schnell Pizzeria Don Camillo
Cuisines: Pizza
Average price: Inexpensive
Area: Gereonsviertel
Address: Friesenstr. 41
50670 Cologne Germany
Phone: 0221 3106811

#447
Altenberger Hof
Cuisines: International
Average price: Modest
Area: Nippes
Address: Mauenheimer Str. 92
50733 Cologne Germany
Phone: 0221 5348077

#448
Fährhaus
Cuisines: Wine Bar, Mediterranean
Average price: Modest
Area: Rodenkirchen
Address: Steinstr. 1
50996 Cologne Germany
Phone: 0221 9359969

#449
Supermercato Biagini
Cuisines: Italian, Grocery
Average price: Modest
Area: Neuehrenfeld
Address: Liebigstr. 163
50823 Cologne Germany
Phone: 0221 9171760

#450
Restaurant Thormann
Cuisines: German
Average price: Expensive
Area: Südstadt
Address: Elsaßstr. 4
50677 Cologne Germany
Phone: 0221 3104491

#451
Marx & Engels
Cuisines: Burgers
Average price: Modest
Area: Belgisches Viertel
Address: Hohenzollernring 21 - 23
50672 Cologne Germany
Phone: 0221 16948299

#452
Plomari
Cuisines: Greek
Average price: Expensive
Area: Sülz
Address: Sülzgürtel 96
50937 Cologne Germany
Phone: 0221 448689

#453
Meister Gerhard
Cuisines: Tapas/Small Plates
Average price: Modest
Area: Südstadt
Address: Chlodwigplatz 6
50678 Cologne Germany
Phone: 0221 92366999

#454
Café Dein & Mein
Cuisines: Cafe
Average price: Exclusive
Area: Agnesviertel
Address: Ewaldistr. 18
50670 Cologne Germany
Phone: 0221 29889715

#455
Pizza Hot
Cuisines: Pizza
Average price: Modest
Area: Dellbrück
Address: Dellbrücker Hauptstr. 151
51069 Cologne Germany
Phone: 0221 6085040

#456
Alteburger Hof
Cuisines: German, International
Average price: Modest
Area: Südstadt
Address: Alteburger Str. 15
50678 Cologne Germany
Phone: 0175 7979488

#457
Balthasar
Cuisines: Cafe, Cocktail Bar, International
Average price: Expensive
Area: Belgisches Viertel
Address: Aachener Str. 18
50674 Cologne Germany
Phone: 0221 16843438

#458
Jogi Sushi
Cuisines: Sushi Bar, Japanese
Average price: Modest
Area: Georgsviertel
Address: Mühlenbach 7
50676 Cologne Germany
Phone: 0221 93112184

#459
Café Schnurrke
Cuisines: Cafe
Average price: Modest
Area: Eigelstein
Address: Ritterstr. 27
50668 Cologne Germany
Phone: 0221 84617980

#460
Falafel König
Cuisines: Middle Eastern
Average price: Inexpensive
Area: Ehrenfeld
Address: Venloer Str. 392
50823 Cologne Germany
Phone: 0221 16899161

#461
Nehring
Cuisines: Food Stand
Average price: Inexpensive
Area: Kwatier Latäng
Address: Zülpicher Platz 4
50674 Cologne Germany
Phone: 0221 2404299

#462
Antica Roma
Cuisines: Italian
Average price: Modest
Area: Wahnheide
Address: Heidestr. 238
51147 Cologne Germany
Phone: 02203 -1835971

#463
Deutzer Fischhaus
Cuisines: Seafood, Fishmonger
Average price: Modest
Area: Deutz
Address: Tempelstr. 7
50679 Cologne Germany
Phone: 0221 98944665

#464
Dicker Hund
Cuisines: Barbeque, American
Average price: Modest
Area: Agnesviertel
Address: Neusser Str. 87
50670 Cologne Germany
Phone: 0221 27077260

#465
Taku
Cuisines: Asian Fusion, Dim Sum
Average price: Exclusive
Area: Gereonsviertel
Address: Trankgasse 1-5
50667 Cologne Germany
Phone: 0221 2703910

#466
Wirtshaus Spitz
Cuisines: German
Average price: Modest
Area: Agnesviertel
Address: Neusser Str. 23
50670 Cologne Germany
Phone: 0221 16864844

#467
Café Orlando
Cuisines: Cafe, Breakfast & Brunch
Average price: Modest
Area: Kwatier Latäng
Address: Engelbertstr. 9
50674 Cologne Germany
Phone: 0221 44909010

#468
Törtchen Törtchen
Cuisines: Cafe, Desserts,
Patisserie/Cake Shop
Average price: Expensive
Area: Apostelnviertel
Address: Apostelnstr. 19
50667 Cologne Germany
Phone: 0221 27253081

#469
Brauhaus Sion
Cuisines: Gastropub
Average price: Modest
Area: Martinsviertel
Address: Unter Taschenmacher 5-7
50667 Cologne Germany
Phone: 0221 2578540

#470
Kulisse
Cuisines: Cafe
Average price: Inexpensive
Area: Kalk
Address: Kalk-Mülheimer Str. 58
51103 Cologne Germany
Phone: 0221 8701125

#471
Neoneo
Cuisines: Pizza, Italian
Average price: Inexpensive
Area: Gereonsviertel
Address: Friesenwall 81
50672 Cologne Germany
Phone: 0176 23548413

#472
China Imbiss Berlin
Cuisines: Chinese
Average price: Inexpensive
Area: Bilderstöckchen
Address: Liebigstr. 257
50739 Cologne Germany
Phone: 0221 1703416

#473
Traubenzeit
Cuisines: European, Wine Bar
Average price: Expensive
Area: Neuehrenfeld
Address: Hauffstr. 1
50825 Cologne Germany
Phone: 0221 2053446

#474
La Patata La Plata
Cuisines: Spanish
Average price: Modest
Area: Südstadt
Address: Kurfürstenstr. 24
50678 Cologne Germany
Phone: 0221 316902

#475
Cafecafe
Cuisines: Cafe, Breakfast & Brunch
Average price: Modest
Area: Ehrenfeld
Address: Venloer Str. 206
50823 Cologne Germany
Phone: 0221 16922523

#476
Hans Im Glück
Cuisines: Burgers, Cocktail Bar
Average price: Modest
Area: Lindenthal
Address: Dürener Str. 122
50931 Cologne Germany
Phone: 0221 94194211

#477
Woyton
Cuisines: Cafe
Average price: Modest
Area: Martinsviertel
Address: In Der Höhle 6
50667 Cologne Germany
Phone: 0221 7596306

#478
d/\blju 'W'
Cuisines: German
Average price: Expensive
Area: Cäcilienviertel
Address: Kaygasse 2
50676 Cologne Germany
Phone: 0221 20080

#479
Da Mé Primi é Vini
Cuisines: Italian
Average price: Expensive
Area: Neumarkt Viertel
Address: Neue Langgasse 4
50667 Cologne Germany
Phone: 0221 27744099

#480
Avila Tapas Bar
Cuisines: Spanish, Tapas Bar
Average price: Modest
Area: Agnesviertel
Address: Krefelder Str. 37
50670 Cologne Germany
Phone: 0221 30197690

#481
Printen Schmitz
Cuisines: Patisserie/Cake Shop, Cafe
Average price: Inexpensive
Area: Neumarkt Viertel
Address: Breite Str. 87 - 91
50667 Cologne Germany
Phone: 0221 2576384

#482
Veedel Vital
Cuisines: Bistro, Cafe, Salad
Average price: Modest
Area: Südstadt
Address: Ubierring 18
50678 Cologne Germany
Phone: 0176 61921716

#483
Coco's Tradition Thai Kitchen
Cuisines: Thai
Average price: Inexpensive
Area: Gereonsviertel
Address: Friesenstr. 77 - 81
50670 Cologne Germany
Phone: 0171 5688164

#484
Taverna Candia
Cuisines: Greek
Average price: Modest
Area: Belgisches Viertel
Address: Brüsseler Str. 70
50674 Cologne Germany
Phone: 0221 518474

#485
Viet Küche
Cuisines: Vietnamese, Cuban
Average price: Inexpensive
Area: Kunibertsviertel
Address: Thürmchenswall 62
50668 Cologne Germany
Phone: 0221 29010259

#486
Scampino
Cuisines: Seafood
Average price: Expensive
Area: Mülheim
Address: Deutz-Mülheimer Str. 199
51063 Cologne Germany
Phone: 0221 618544

#487
HoteLux
Cuisines: Bar, Russian
Average price: Modest
Area: Deutz
Address: Von-Sandt-Platz 10
50679 Cologne Germany
Phone: 0221 241136

#488
Lindenthal by Schneiders
Cuisines: Bar, Fondue, Italian
Average price: Expensive
Area: Lindenthal
Address: Lindenthalgürtel 31
50935 Cologne Germany
Phone: 0221 9903404

#489
Tutto
Cuisines: Italian, Pizza
Average price: Inexpensive
Area: Neumarkt Viertel
Address: Kreuzgasse 2 - 4
50677 Cologne Germany
Phone: 0221 54816461

#490
Yogissimo
Cuisines: Ice Cream & Frozen Yogurt,
Coffee & Tea, Waffles
Average price: Modest
Area: Ehrenfeld
Address: Venloer Str. 348
50823 Cologne Germany
Phone: 0221 16914595

#491
Cottas
Cuisines: International, Cafe, Cocktail Bar
Average price: Modest
Area: Lindenthal
Address: Dürener Str. 87
50931 Cologne Germany
Phone: 0221 407009

#492
Collina's
Cuisines: Italian
Average price: Expensive
Area: Martinsviertel
Address: Am Hof 48
50667 Cologne Germany
Phone: 0221 32091901

#493
Antep Sultan Sofrasi
Cuisines: Turkish
Average price: Modest
Area: Sülz
Address: Weißhausstr. 27
50937 Cologne Germany
Phone: 0221 88820997

#494
Bei Lena
Cuisines: German, Pubs
Average price: Inexpensive
Area: Belgisches Viertel
Address: Hansaring 19
50670 Cologne Germany
Phone: 0163 7747062

#495
Yay Trong Kham Korat
Cuisines: Thai
Average price: Inexpensive
Area: Severinsviertel
Address: Severinstr. 193
50678 Cologne Germany
Phone: 0221 27847583

#496
Vier Jahreszeiten
Cuisines: Bistro, Organic Stores
Average price: Modest
Area: Martinsviertel
Address: Herzogstr. 34
50667 Cologne Germany
Phone: 0221 99554833

#497
Ponchos
Cuisines: Argentine, Steakhouse
Average price: Expensive
Area: Martinsviertel
Address: Salzgasse 11
50667 Cologne Germany
Phone: 0221 2772999

#498
La Gazetta
Cuisines: Pubs, Seafood
Average price: Modest
Area: Gereonsviertel
Address: An den Dominikanern 4
50668 Cologne Germany
Phone: 0221 1644470

#499
Le Bistrot 99
Cuisines: French, Bistro
Average price: Modest
Area: Junkersdorf
Address: Aachener Str. 1002
50858 Cologne Germany
Phone: 0221 17044392

#500
Weltmeister Grill
Cuisines: Curry Sausage, Fast Food
Average price: Modest
Area: Belgisches Viertel
Address: Maybachstr. 30
50670 Cologne Germany
Phone: 0177 2144441

Printed in Great Britain
by Amazon